Reading Wo
Everyday Wo

LEVEL 6

GW01397974

Lineo

Frances Cross

Series Editor – Jean Conteh

MACMILLAN

To the Teacher
or Parent

This is a fictional story set in the mountains of Lesotho, in southern Africa. It is about a family who have to leave their home because the government want to build a dam. But Lineo does not want to leave the only home she and her family have ever known. Both boys and girls will enjoy this story, and learn some lessons from it about the importance of our homes and families.

The story is divided into six chapters.

The book is meant for the children to read on their own. The language is simple, and the pictures will help them to understand the story.

Use the book in this way:

• Before the children begin to read this book, ask them what they think the title means, and what they think the book might be about.

• Talk about the importance of water with the children, why we need it and what we use it for.

• Make sure that the children know what a dam is, and talk about how dams can help to generate electricity and improve water supplies, but also how they can destroy villages and land.

• Let the children read the book by themselves. Encourage them to ask for help if they have difficulties.

• When the children have finished reading, ask them if they enjoyed the story. Ask them to turn to pages 47–48, where there are some questions and activities to help them understand the story better.

Above all, let the children enjoy reading this book. Then they will want to read more, and will develop into independent readers.

Chapter 1

An important meeting

It was late afternoon in the mountains of Lesotho. It had been a beautiful, sunny day. An eagle soared high in the sky, his wings spread wide. Lineo and her sister Elizabeth were collecting the dry washing from the rotary washing line outside their rondavel*.

The rotary washing line was a special present from their father to their mother. He had carried it proudly over the Caledon River bridge when he came home from the South African mines for one of his visits.

---

*A *rondavel* is a round house with a thatched grass roof.

Suddenly, Elizabeth said, 'Look! There's somebody coming to see us.'

Both girls peered down from the mountainside to the floor of the valley where a Basotho* pony was walking, sure-footed, along the stony path.

A man sat on the pony. He was wearing a traditional hat and was wrapped in a Basotho blanket. He was so far away that it was hard to see who it was.

The girls went on looking down at the man on the pony. Slowly, they began to recognise the way he was sitting on the pony, and the way he held his head.

'It's Father!' Lineo said, excitedly. 'Father's coming home for a visit.'

The girls ran home to tell Mother, Granny and Aunty Mafusi.

Everybody ran outside the rondavel to see. The man sat comfortably as the little pony walked steadily along the floor of the valley. The family at the top of the mountain watched with interest. Then, Lineo heard her mother, Malineo, whisper quietly to Aunty Mafusi.

'I hope everything is all right. Thabo was not supposed to come back from the mine until later in the month. Maybe he is sick.'

'No,' Aunty Mafusi whispered back. 'I don't think he's sick. Look how well he sits on the pony. He couldn't sit like that if he were sick.'

Eventually, Lineo's father arrived at the homestead. Everybody crowded round and greeted him with pleasure.

Basotho is the name we give to the men of Lesotho. Basotho ponies are the small horses they ride.

Malineo said to her daughters, 'You children, go and help Aunty and Granny to prepare some food. We must make some crispy dough cakes for your father, as he'll be hungry.'

Lineo and Elizabeth went in to the little cooking rondavel to help their grandmother. After a while their parents joined them. Thabo sat on a bench and Malineo sat on the ground with her legs stretched out in front of her. Aunty Mafusi sat with them.

As she helped her granny, Lineo listened to what her parents were saying.

'I've come home now because the Chief has called a very important meeting,' her father said. 'It's a meeting to talk about something that will change all our lives.'

Lineo was upset to hear her father speaking like this. She noticed that he looked worried. She wondered what was happening.

'Thabo, what is this important change?' her mother asked.

Her husband didn't answer for a moment, and then he said something Lineo couldn't hear. And, after that, she had to help her granny, so she didn't hear any more of the important conversation between her parents.

That evening, as always, Granny told stories after supper. They all sat and listened. Granny was one of the best storytellers in the area, and some of her ghost stories were very frightening!

Lineo and Elizabeth would curl up closer and closer to her when she told the ghost stories.

But, today, Granny wasn't telling a ghost story.

She was telling the story of the first King Moshoeshoe, who founded the Basotho nation. Of course, they knew this story very well. They had heard it many times before. But, when Granny told it, the story came alive. They could clearly see it in their own minds.

At the end of the story, Granny said, 'This is how this ordinary man called Moshoeshoe became a leader of his people. The Boers* in South Africa were chasing these people. It was a very dangerous time, and everybody was afraid. But Moshoeshoe was clever, because he found the safest place in Africa to hide. He led everyone to the great rock fortress of Thaba Bosiu in the Maluti Mountains. Nobody could catch them there. And it was in that very place that he founded the Basotho Kingdom. And, in time, he became a great and wise king, much respected by everyone.'

---

* The *Boers* were white farmers in South Africa who originally came from the Netherlands, in Europe.

When Granny finished her story, Lineo realised that everybody had been listening to it very carefully, even her aunty and father and mother. It made Lineo feel proud to be part of such a wonderful kingdom.

The next morning, when Lineo woke up, her aunty said, 'Your father has gone for an important meeting with the Chief. Go and wake up Elizabeth, because it will soon be time for you to walk to school.'

Lineo woke Elizabeth.

Soon, the two girls were walking round the mountainside to school. It was a long walk, which took them an hour, and it was always in the shade, not in the sun.

They met Mpai, Lineo's best friend. Mpai smiled when she saw Lineo walking up with Elizabeth.

'Why doesn't the sun come round this side of the mountain?' Elizabeth said.

'Never mind,' Lineo said. 'It's cooler in the shade.'

As they walked along, Lineo thought about her father and wondered what was happening at the meeting.

Lineo told Mpai about her father coming home.

'I've heard something is happening, too,' Mpai said, 'but I don't know exactly what it is. My uncle came home yesterday and he looked very serious.'

The two girls tried to think what was going on, but they couldn't decide.

'It's no use, worrying,' said Lineo. 'We'll know soon enough.'

Lineo's father came back from the meeting that evening. Like Mpai's uncle, he looked serious. The next day, he rode back down the mountain, and Lineo was no wiser.

Chapter 2

Where will they build
the dams?

Three weeks later, everybody in the Lesotho
Highlands knew what was happening.

Malineo called Lineo and Elizabeth together and
said, 'You know your father came three weeks ago. Well I
can tell you now why he had to come. There is going to
be a big scheme here in the mountains to make
electricity, mainly for South Africa and for Lesotho.'

She paused and the girls looked at her. Their eyes
were wide.

'The scheme will be powered by water,' she said.

'There is water here to do that,' said Lineo.

'Yes,' agreed her mother, 'they will have to build two or three big dams so that they can hold the water in them.'

'Where will they build these dams?' asked Elizabeth.

'Here. They will build them here,' said her mother.

There was a silence for a moment, as the girls tried to understand what their mother was telling them.

Then, Lineo said, 'How can they build the dams here?'

And when Malineo turned to look at her daughter, Lineo saw that her mother's eyes were filled with tears.

'By flooding the whole area,' Malineo said. 'Our home, and the homes of our friends will all be under water.'

Elizabeth was shocked.

'But what will we do?' she asked. 'Where can we go if our home is under water?'

'The government will find us new houses. They say they will build us better houses and our lives will be much better. And they will give us some money,' said Malineo, in a sad voice.

'But if we leave here,' Lineo said, 'and they flood the valley, the bones of our ancestors will be drowned.'

'I know,' said her mother, sounding worried. 'They say they will take up the bones of the ancestors and bury them somewhere else, but we will not be able to find many of them. They are in unmarked graves.'

She was very unhappy.

Later on, Lineo talked to her granny about the flooding.

'I don't think the thing they are doing is right,' said Granny. 'But I am an old person and maybe I don't understand these things. I believe that, if we flood the valley, we'll find that the ancestors grow angry and bring bad luck on us. Also I believe that the life of the Basotho people will change if this happens. If we move away from our traditional villages and go to live in another place, I think this will be the end of our special way of life.'

Lineo felt frightened when she thought about how everything she knew would change.

She loved her home, and didn't want to move anywhere else.

She felt the same way as Granny. Even though Granny said that Lineo's father would be able to stay with them when they moved to their new house, and he would not have to travel any more to work on the mines in South Africa, she didn't want to move.

Lineo didn't want to move, even when Granny told her there would be enough money to build a nice new house with a flat roof and several rooms.

Chapter 3

Money or land?

For the next few months, all the people in the Highlands wondered what would happen. It was the only thing that they talked about. Some of the Basotho people were very unhappy about the water scheme.

This included the local sangoma*. Like Lineo and her granny, he believed that disturbing the bones of the ancestors was a very bad thing to do. He was also upset because an important and rare plant would be drowned under the water. It was a special aloe that grew on the mountainside. He used it for healing.

But some people, especially the younger ones, thought that the scheme was a good idea. It would bring many good things. The husbands and fathers would no longer need to work far away on the mines in South Africa. They could stay with their families. The compensation** money would mean they could build new and better homes.

And so people were divided in the way they felt. Even Lineo's family couldn't agree about whether the new scheme would be good or not. Her mother did not want to leave her home and home village. She had lived all her life there.

But Lineo's father believed that the change would improve their lives. The village they would be moved to had a better school with more facilities. He would be able to build a nicer home for them.

The men in charge of building the dams for the water tried very hard to listen to the worries and anxieties of the Basotho people. They sent many experts to talk to them. A man came from England to speak to the people about the new village they would go to. He talked for a long time, and he told them a lot of good things. The villagers listened to him in silence.

---

* A *sangoma* is a traditional healer and wise man or woman.
** *Compensation* is money paid to the people in return for loss – in this story, it is for losing their houses and land.

But then one of the villagers said, 'I do not see how I can make a living if you take my land away from me. I won't have wild vegetables, which I get free. I won't have potatoes, which I get free. I won't have beans, maize and cow's milk, which are all free. I won't have my chicken house and my chickens and my rondavel.'

Many of the other villagers nodded in agreement. They thought that if they gave away their land, they would not be able to live as they had before. The Basotho people believed that having money was not as valuable as having land. The man from England did not know what to say in reply.

Chapter 4

Lineo runs away

Several months went by. There were many meetings between the planners and the Basotho people.

'You will know the decision soon,' the planners promised.

The following week, they told the families in Lineo's village and the three next to it that they would have to move. The people began to pack up their belongings.

Lineo couldn't believe that she would lose her home. She couldn't bear to think that soon it would be under water, that she would never see it again. She couldn't bear to think she wouldn't be able to go to her favourite places, like the little tree next to the big stone, where she and Elizabeth liked to sit in the evenings.

They would not be able to play the lesokoana* game with the girls in the next village.

Her father had gone back to the mine, but he was coming home in a few days to help with the move.

'I don't like all these changes,' grumbled Lineo's Granny. 'I'm too old for changes.'

Lineo gazed at Granny's stooped back, and her eyes filled with tears. She felt so sad for her.

'The government shouldn't have sent us away from our home,' she said.

'Well, there's nothing we can do,' said Granny.

But, two days before they left the village, Lineo decided that there was something she could do. She could run away. She would hide in the mountains and nobody would find her.

They would go to the new village without her.

Lineo waited until it was dark and everybody was fast asleep. Then she crept out of the rondavel.

It was quite dark outside, but there were some stars in the sky to keep her company.

---

*The lesokoana game came from a time when there was drought, and the girls from one village stole the Chief's cooking stick (the lesokoana) from another village. The girls from this village chased the 'thieves' and had a tug of war with them to claim the stick back. They believed that the gods would send rain for them, as they had sweated so much on the dry land.

She went down to her favourite place where, close to the tree, there was a little cave with dinosaur footprints on the walls. She wrapped her blanket around her and tried to sleep. She imagined the old dinosaurs roaming the area thousands of years before.

She decided that in the morning she would get up very early and find a safe place further up the mountain to hide.

The next morning, before the sun started to climb in the sky, Lineo started her journey.

At home, everybody was very busy getting ready for the move. They soon realised that Lineo was missing.

Malineo said anxiously, 'Where can she be?'

'She won't be far away,' said Granny, reassuringly. 'You finish getting everything ready. I'll go with Elizabeth to look for her. Don't worry. We'll be back very soon.'

She patted Malineo's hand, but Malineo still looked very worried.

Granny and Elizabeth left the village and went to look
for Lineo. They searched everywhere but they couldn't
find her. They went to all her favourite places, but there
was no sign of her.

'Do you know where your sister has gone?' said
Granny, sounding worried.

'No, I don't know,' said Elizabeth, who was beginning to get worried about Lineo as well.

'We'll have to go back to the others soon,' said Granny. 'What can we do if we don't find her?'

And she went on calling Lineo in her cracked old voice.

Another half hour went by, with no sign of Lineo. By now, they were quite far from their own village and Granny was very anxious.

'We'll have to go back to the house,' she said, wearily, 'I don't know what else we can do.'

Sadly, they turned to start the walk back to their home. They reached the top of a ridge, and Elizabeth turned around to have one more look at the valley behind them.

'Granny, look! Over there!' she cried, pointing towards what looked like a crumpled pile of clothes on the ground.

Granny turned to look.

'It's Lineo!' she said. 'Quickly – come with me!'

They scrambled down the slope towards Lineo, as quickly as they could, both terrified about what they would find when they reached Lineo. It seemed to take so long to reach her – and what would they find when they did?

At last, they reached her. She was lying on a rock, quite still and silent.

Elizabeth began to cry.

'Granny, she isn't moving – I think she's dead,' she said. 'Look, she has a big bump on the side of her head. She must have fallen.'

Granny knelt down by Lineo's side and, very carefully, looked at her head. It was swollen and red on one side where she had fallen. Elizabeth stared at her sister, unhappy and frightened. Granny felt Lineo's neck, to see if she could feel a pulse – a sign that Lineo's heart was still beating and she was still alive.

Eventually, she felt it. It was weak, but it was there.

'Lineo isn't dead, Elizabeth,' she said, with relief. 'She must have lost consciousness when she fell.'

She smiled faintly at Elizabeth.

'Now, you must stop crying and help me. I want you to go back home as quickly as you can and get help. I know you will do this well, because you are a very grown-up and sensible girl. Quick, now.'

Elizabeth stopped crying and did as she was asked. A few minutes later, she was climbing the ridge and was soon out of sight.

Granny was alone on the mountain.

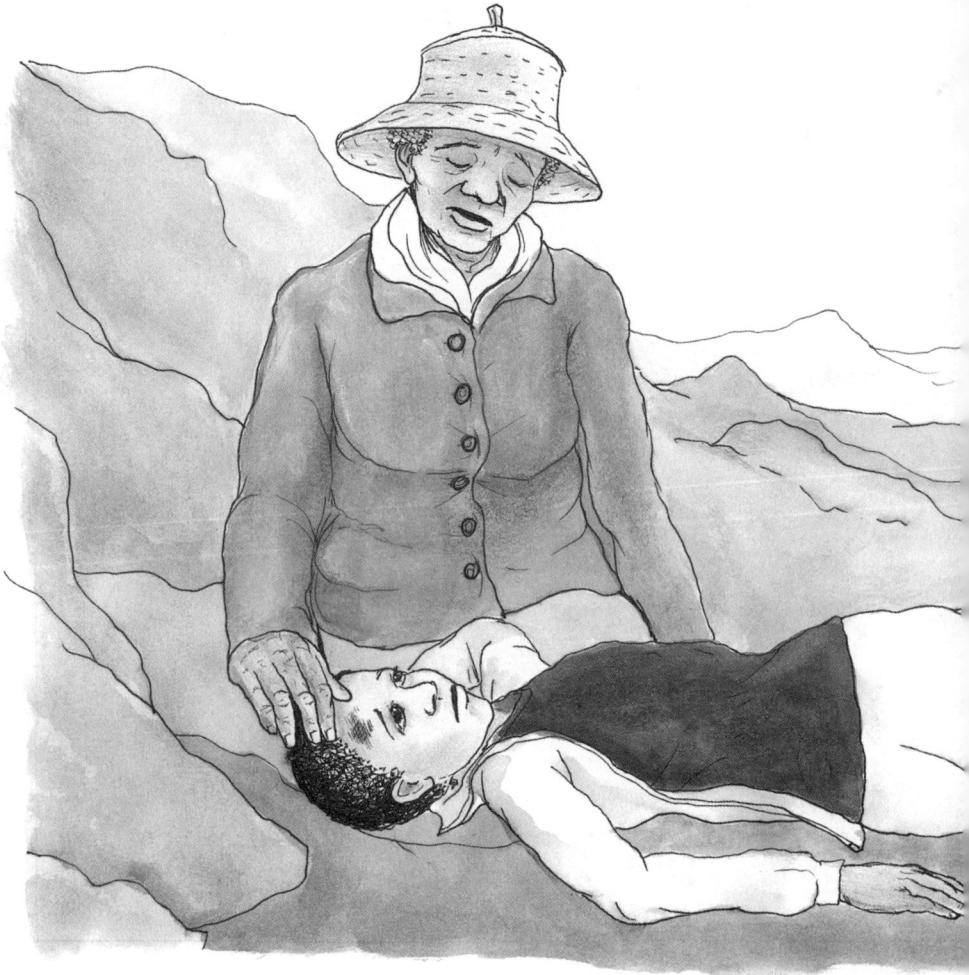

Granny sat close by her granddaughter, gently stroking her head. She wasn't afraid of being alone on the mountainside. This was her home, the place where she felt safest in the whole world. She looked down at Lineo and was thankful that they had found her.

She had been sitting there peacefully for a few moments when Lineo stirred. She began to wake up, and struggled to move.

'Stay still,' said Granny. 'You had a bad bang on your head when you fell. Just lie there. Elizabeth has gone to get some help.'

Gently she stroked Lineo's face and sighed.

'Lineo, what a lot of trouble you have caused. Why did you leave the village?' Granny asked.

Lineo's eyes filled with tears.

She looked up at her frail old grandmother, feeling her rough hand gently stroking her forehead, and said, 'Granny, I just couldn't bear to leave the village. It's our home.'

Lineo began to sob.

Granny went on looking at her, her old eyes full of kindness. She didn't say anything for a moment.

Then she said, 'Yes, it is our home. But we do not have a choice, Lineo. Sometimes in this world, things happen which we can't control.'

Granny was speaking very quietly and softly.

She went on, 'This is one of those times. It would be wonderful to stay here in our special place with all our neighbours and friends around us, and our rondavels, and our mealie patch, and our little peach tree. But it's not possible.'

Granny stopped for a moment, her own eyes filling with tears.

Then she said, 'I feel very sad about this move too. But we must not forget one very important thing.'

'What's that?' asked Lineo.

'That we still have our family. That's the main thing. We will all move together and start up somewhere else and it will be all right. We'll get to know new neighbours and soon they'll be as special as the ones we have now. An old lady I met the other day told me that she had moved about ten times in her life, and she seemed quite happy.'

Granny paused again for a moment.

'The thing you have to remember,' she said, 'is that we must all help each other the best way we can. I know you didn't mean to worry your parents and me and Elizabeth, but do you see how much trouble you have caused by running away?'

Lineo's eyes filled with tears again.

'I'm sorry,' she said, taking hold of Granny's hand and holding it tight, 'I've been selfish. You are right. I shouldn't have run away. If you can manage to face this move, I should be able to.'

They stayed together quietly on the side of the mountain, until they saw the figures of Lineo's parents, followed by Elizabeth, racing down towards them.

Chapter 5

We mustn't worry

For the next two days, Lineo felt quite weak, and her head hurt. She sat quietly near her grandmother, helping her with small tasks. Her parents did not scold her, because she had been hurt. Instead, they were very kind to her.

The next day was the day before they were going to leave the village, Lineo's father said, 'Listen, everyone. I am going to hear Ntate Molati. He wants to speak to us. He is in our neighbour's homestead.'

Ntate Molati was a very respected man in the village. He had been a teacher before he retired and he had read a lot of books.

Everybody wanted to go and hear Ntate Molati, and Lineo said she was strong enough to walk there as well.

When they arrived, several other people were standing around waiting to hear Ntate Molati.

He soon arrived.

He had come because he had found something out about people in Great Britain whose homes were flooded. Everyone gathered to listen to Ntate Molati.

'Yesterday, I found out some information about a place where the people lost their village,' he said. 'It was a long time ago, in the 1950s, and the whole village was flooded, and everything, even the cemetery, went under water.'

Ntate Molati stopped speaking and stared seriously over his glasses at the people in front of him.

'This thing was not happening in our country, but in Wales, which is a country that is part of Great Britain.'

He paused and then added, 'The bad thing was that many people became upset after this had happened. They suffered because they had allowed their homes to be flooded, and some saw ghosts of those who were buried in the cemetery.'

There was a murmuring among the people.

The Basotho people revere their ancestors, and they become very worried if they think their ancestors will be displeased.

'What happened in the end?' asked one villager.

Ntate Molati shook his head gravely.

'In the end, the people accepted their new lives. But some of the villagers never got over the sadness of what had happened, and many of the people felt angry for a long time, especially since those who used the electricity generated by the water from the dam lived in England, and Wales is a different country from England.'

Everybody looked at each other sadly.

'But there is nothing we can do,' said Malineo, at last. 'We are leaving here tomorrow. There is nothing we can do. The government will not let us stay here any longer.'

Ntate Molati nodded gravely.

'Then we must pray to God that the ancestors will not become angry when we leave this place,' he said, 'and we must pray that God is good to us in the new place.'

He finished speaking and everybody moved away, talking amongst themselves. Ntate Molati's story about the people in Wales worried them, but his last words comforted them a little.

'Now then, my family,' said Lineo's father, quietly, as they went back to the rondavel. 'We must think very carefully about what Ntate Molati has said. We must pray, and we must not worry.'

But no one could help thinking about families so far away, having the same experience of losing their homes and feeling sad in the same way that they did.

'We must be happy now, though,' said Lineo's father, firmly, as they gathered the last of their things together to move the next morning.

And so the family moved their belongings to the new house with the flat roof in another valley quite far away. The girls went to a new school and Lineo's father stayed at home all the time. He made a big farm and grew a lot of things for them to eat. And, although it was a different life, it wasn't too bad. And, gradually, they began to get to know their neighbours and their life began to settle down again.

Chapter 6

The new dam

One day, more than a year later, Lineo's father took his family back to the place where their village had been.

Now it was under water, far under water, and a huge dam stood in the valley, from one ridge to the next. It was an amazing-looking dam, with the water pouring down one side of it in a great, gushing waterfall. Above the dam was a huge lake.

Lineo looked down into the lake, and all she could think was that, far underneath the water, lay her old home, and that she would never see it again.

She felt very sad and there were tears in her eyes. She wondered what the people in Wales must have felt like when they first saw the water covering their village.

Then she realised that Granny was standing next to her, holding her hand.

'It is sad,' said Granny. 'It is sad to see everything of the past disappeared in such a way.'

Lineo turned to look at the old lady and saw she had tears in her eyes.

'It's very sad,' said Lineo.

Granny smiled at her. 'Yes, it is. But do you remember our conversation on the mountainside when you fell and hurt your head. Do you remember what I said?'

Lineo stared back at her Granny. She walked down the mountain a little way. She picked up a stone and threw it into the water below.

Then, after a moment, she said, 'Yes, I remember. You told me that sometimes it's not possible to control things, and that sometimes things happen which we can't control. And that when this happens there is nothing we can do except accept them.'

Granny smiled again.

'I think we can manage to do that,' she said. 'Don't you?'

'I think so too,' said Lineo, 'but I hope we're not like the old lady who you met who moved ten times!'

And Granny and Lineo laughed.

Malineo heard Lineo and Granny laughing together and turned to look at them. She was glad to hear that they were not too sad any more.

'I don't think we should stand here and look at all this water when there is so much to do at home,' she said to the family. 'Why don't we go back home and make some nice food, and maybe we can ask the neighbours to share it with us.'

And, with that, the family turned away from the dam and walked together back to their new home.

Have you seen a dam before? Here are some photos of dams in different parts of Africa. Look in an atlas to see where each country is.

This dam is called the Aswan High Dam. It is in Egypt.

This dam is called the Kariba Dam. It is between Zambia and Zimbabwe.

This dam is called the Akosombo Dam. It is in Ghana.

2   What was the name of the first King of the Basotho nation? Look on page 8 to remind yourself. Look in your history book to find out what you can about the Basotho people. Write a few sentences about them.

3   Why did the government of Lesotho want to build the dams? Find out what you can about dams and write a report about them. Write about the advantages as well as the disadvantages.

4   At the end of Chapter 3, the visitor from England did not know what to say to the people. Do you think he understood their fears? If you were the visitor, what would you say to the people? Write out what you would say.

5   What made Granny most sad about the move from the old village? What did she think might happen when the family moved? Imagine that you are Granny, and you are trying to explain to the visitor from England why you are sad. Write down what you would say.

6   With your classmates, make a short play where Granny and the visitor talk about the new dams. One person can be Granny. Another person can be the visitor. Other people can take the parts of others in the story, such as Lineo, Elizabeth and their parents.

7   When Granny and Elizabeth first found Lineo, Granny was very careful not to move Lineo's head. Why do you think she was careful? What else did she do to look after Lineo? Try to find out as much as you can about First Aid, so that you could help if somebody has an accident.

8   Imagine that you are Lineo, and that two years have passed since you moved to your new village. Write about the things you like in your new village, and the things you liked about your old village.